T0113181

THE TURN OF THE SCREWDRIVER

50 DARK & TWISTED *Literary Cocktails*
Inspired by **ANNE RICE, MARY SHELLEY,**
EDGAR ALLAN POE
& Other Legendary Gothic Authors

IPHIGENIA JONES

Published by:
Ulysses Press
PO Box 3440
Berkeley, CA 94703
www.ulyssespress.com

ISBN: 978-1-64604-681-2
Library of Congress Control Number: 2024931677

Printed in China
10 9 8 7 6 5 4 3 2 1

Project editor: Shelona Belfon
Managing editor: Claire Chun
Editor: Renee Rutledge
Proofreader: Paula Dragosh
Front cover design: Akangksha Sarmah
Interior design and layout: Winnie Liu
Photography: Nevyana Dimitrova
Images: front cover illustrations from Freepik; pink borders © Giraphics/shutterstock.com

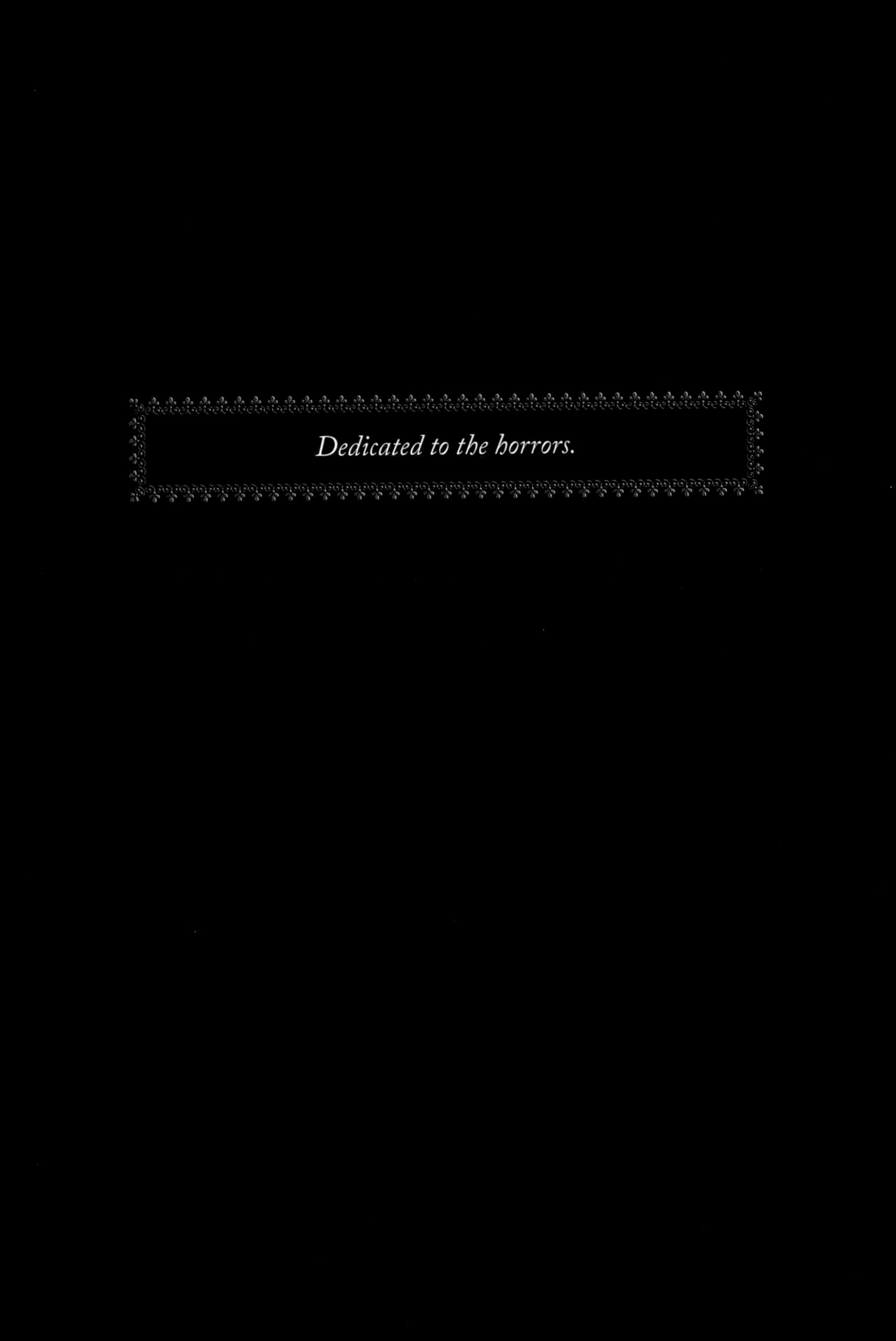

Dedicated to the horrors.

CONTENTS

THE MODERN (1970–2022)

INTRODUCTION

It was a dark and stormy night.

What a delightful way to begin a spooky story sure to tingle your spine. It comes from an 1830s novel by Edward Bulwer-Lytton and has been used to frighten (and amuse) ever since. Lucky for us, a "dark and stormy" also happens to be the name of a cocktail.

There is something about gothic literature that pairs nicely with a well-made drink. Perhaps it is the atmosphere of a cold drink in one hand while a storm rages in the novel, or the bitterness of alcohol paired with a doomed protagonist's regret, or maybe it is the liquid courage we need in order to dare turn the pages. In this book, we will provide the absolute best pairings of book and cocktail to enhance the experience of these famous tales.

Like an undead creature, the genre of gothic literature continues to haunt us. It is a massive genre, which contains not only classic stories of ghosts and creatures but also gothic romance, Southern gothic, and dozens of other subgenres. Gothic literature may have begun with *The Castle of Otranto* by Horace Walpole in 1764, but it has remained relevant ever since. From the paranoid stories of Poe to the windswept romances of the Brontës to the blood-soaked books of Anne Rice, it is a genre that always grows and changes. It accepts the trends of the moment to reflect the current fears of society.

I have attempted to pay homage to not only the age-old and familiar stories but some of the newer gothic masterpieces from authors such as Carmen Maria Machado and Elizabeth Hand. This is by no means a definitive list of all the gothic literature in existence, just this author's careful selection from an ever-growing list of scarily delightful stories. Notably, not all of gothic literature fits in this recipe book. Some of the most influential gothic authors, such as Toni Morrison or Rivers Solomon, feature books with serious themes of slavery and generational racism that are absolutely essential but should be read with a clear mind and open heart and are perhaps not suited to this book's more whimsical take on the genre. There may be more stories and books you wish to see represented in these pages, but alas, time constrains us all.

So settle in, open a book, and take a sip. Try not to be terrified.

BAR BASICS

Let's review some of the bar basics needed to make the spookiest spirits for your enjoyment.

GLASSWARE

COCKTAIL (OR MARTINI) GLASS: This classic V-shaped stemmed glass is the go-to choice for drinks that are shaken or stirred and served "up" without ice.

COLLINS OR HIGHBALL GLASS: A tall cylindrical glass reserved for drinks served over ice (otherwise known as "rocks"). The Collins is taller than a highball and usually used for drinks that are filled with some bubbly on top.

COUPE GLASS: A squat wide-stemmed glass with an iconic shape used for many classic cocktails. This will give some old-school glamour to your drink.

COPPER MUG: The metallic standard for the Moscow mule. It is literally just a copper coffee mug.

MUG: This plain version of its copper cousin is used for hot drinks.

PINT GLASS: A tall tapered glass usually used for beer and some cocktails.

ROCKS (OR OLD-FASHIONED) GLASS: A short cylindrical tumbler reserved for drinks served over ice.

SHOT GLASS: These tiny drinking vessels are for just what their name suggests: shots. This glass can also be used as a measuring glass.

HURRICANE GLASS: A short-stemmed tall glass with a curved bowl is named after the cocktail that made it famous. It is used for many tropical or frozen drinks.

RED WINE GLASS: A tall, stemmed glass with a curved bowl and a wide mouth.

WHITE WINE GLASS: A slightly smaller relative to the red wine glass but with a narrower mouth.

EQUIPMENT

BLENDER: For frozen drinks when your warm fire is too intense.

JUICER: For freshly juiced lemons and limes (generally preferred over bottled citrus juices).

MEASURING CUPS AND SPOONS: Household staples that are essential for any perfect cocktail creation. Measuring cups can range from

¼ to 1 cup, and larger glass or plastic cups can measure beyond that. Spoons will range from ¼ teaspoon to a tablespoon.

PITCHER AND PUNCH BOWL: For when you mean to entertain a group of people or ghosts, doesn't matter. Any large glass or ceramic pitcher will suffice.

BAR SPOON: A teaspoon with a long handle used for mixing ingredients in tall glasses or shakers.

CORKSCREW: A classic double-hinged wine key is a preferred favorite, but any variety you have works too. Whatever gets you at the precious alcohol faster to stave off those demons.

SHAKER (BOSTON OR COCKTAIL): The finest shakers are metal, which help the drink cool down quickly. A classic cocktail shaker has a built-in strainer and cap, whereas a Boston shaker has a pint glass and a metal cup that fit together.

MIXING GLASS: Any tall glass that you can use to stir ingredients. It can also be the glass pint half of a Boston shaker.

MUDDLER: A wooden or plastic masher used to smash citrus, herbs, or other ingredients against the bottom of the glass. It helps release essential oils and smells that enhance the flavors in your drink and remind you of the happier things in life.

STRAINER: If you use a Boston shaker over a cocktail shaker, you will need to use a strainer to make sure all those undesirable bits don't get into your drink.

JIGGER: The most essential of bar tools. This hourglass-shaped measuring tool usually has 1 ounce on one side and 1.5 ounces on the other, although other size variations are available. Most cocktails—like most stories—are about proportion. Having precise portions of suspense, dread, despair, and hope make a thrilling novel as well as cocktail.

PARING KNIFE AND CUTTING BOARD: For cutting citrus for juicing, garnishing, or twisting.

TECHNIQUES

GARNISHING: Some drinks look awfully bland in their glasses as just a semi-clear liquid with no panache—boring. A garnish adds flair and sophistication to your drink, much the same way that a falling helmet might add impending bodily harm to someone's life. Commonly, garnishes are twists (a peel cut from the skin of a citrus fruit) or a wedge (likewise cut from a citrus fruit). You can also violently skewer a few olives or a cherry bathed in sugar syrup to add as a garnish. Umbrellas in the context of this book should be reserved for protecting you from the constant deluge of rain that's setting the ambience as you read.

MUDDLING: Muddling is the process of smashing fruit, herbs, or sugar to release fresh flavors and infuse them into your drinks. To begin to muddle ingredients for your delicious drink, start by choosing a sturdy glass or cocktail shaker. If you select the wrong glass, you may end up breaking your vessel and wreaking devastation on your poor floors.

Remember to grab your muddler as mentioned above, though the end of a wooden spoon or rolling pin will work in a pinch. Place the ingredients that you wish to muddle into the bottom of the glass. Cut up any pieces of fruit or vegetables in order to make them more manageable. Press down and twist the muddler onto the ingredients in the bottom of the glass. If muddling herbs like mint or basil, take some care. A gentler touch is needed, lest they turn bitter—much like myself.

RIMMING: Don't you love a dramatic presentation? Coating the rim of your cocktail glass with salt or sugar is sure to impress and delight any visitor you may be entertaining. There are a few tried-and-true ways to rim a cocktail, and here is but one humble suggestion. In a saucer slightly larger than the rim of the glass, pour the desired rim ingredient, such as sugar or salt. To moisten the rim of the glass, rub the fleshy side of a citrus wedge (such as lime or lemon) along the rim. Immediately after, hold the glass upside down and dip the rim into the saucer of said ingredient. Press and twist the glass gently to coat the rim before shaking off any excess. Now you're ready to add your darkly decadent drink to a well-dressed glass.

SHAKING: Do you hear that? A strange click-clacking echoing through the halls? Luckily for you, it is only the noise of a well-shaken cocktail. Shaking cocktails will ensure that your drink is perfectly blended, chilled, and aerated. Pour your ingredients along with ice cubes into the shaker. Secure the lid or shaker tin. Hold the shaker in both hands and lift it over your shoulder before shaking vigorously for 10 to 15 seconds.

STIRRING: Ah, stirring. Shaking's gentler sister, required when making a mixed drink directly in the serving glass, or when using ingredients that are primarily spirits. After pouring the ingredients into a glass, select your bar spoon. Hold the spoon between your thumb and forefinger, and between your middle finger and ring finger for more stability. Place the spoon into the glass, keeping the back of the spoon against the walls of the glass. While stirring, the spoon back should always be against the glass. Stir for about 20 to 30 seconds to ensure that the drink is well mixed.

TOPPING OFF: Feel like adding something bubbly to your drink to bring some fleeting joy to your life? That is exactly what topping off does, by adding a few ounces of champagne, club soda, or cream to your drink. The precise amount generally depends on the ratio of liquid to ice in your glass. A variant of topping off is layering, when you pour the ingredient onto the back of a spoon over the drink to evenly distribute it over the drink to create a distinct layered effect.

BREWS

SPIRITS

GIN: A clear distilled spirit primarily made from juniper berries and other botanicals like coriander, citrus peel, and spices. This drink gives some cocktails a needed flavor pop that should revive a dour spirit.

VODKA: A colorless and odorless distilled spirit typically made from fermented grains like wheat, rye, or potatoes. Commonly served straight in some places, this spirit is a mainstay for classic cocktails for its versatility and ability to drown away your sadness.

RUM: A distilled alcoholic beverage made from fermented and distilled sugarcane by-products such as molasses and sugarcane juice. It can vary widely in flavor, from light and subtle to dark and rich, depending on factors like aging and production methods.

WHISKEY: Commonly associated with brooding writers, this distilled spirit is typically made from a fermented grain mash of wheat, corn, rye, and barley. It's aged in wooden barrels, usually oak, which imparts flavors and colors to the final product. Whiskey comes in various styles such as Scotch whisky, bourbon, rye whiskey, and Irish whiskey, each with distinct characteristics—much like the many shades of black in your wardrobe.

TEQUILA: Primarily made from the blue agave plant, native to Mexico, this distilled spirit is known for its distinctive flavor, which can range from earthy and vegetal to fruity and spicy. It comes in several types, including añejo (aged for at least one year), reposado (aged in oak barrels for a few months to a year), and blanco (unaged).

SOTOL: A product of the whimsically named Desert Spoon plant (*Dasylirion wheeleri*) found in northern Mexico and parts of the southwestern United States. It has a unique flavor profile, often described as herbal, earthy, and slightly smoky.

MEZCAL: Unlike tequila, which is made specifically from the blue agave plant, this distilled spirit can be produced from various types of agave, each contributing to its distinct flavor profile.

CACHAÇA: Similar to rum but hailing from Brazil, this distilled spirit is made from sugarcane juice.

ABSINTHE: Mistakenly thought to be a hallucinogen, this highly alcoholic spirit is known for its strong anise flavor and historical association with artists, bohemians, and other sundry peoples. It is distilled with a variety of botanicals, including wormwood, which gives it a distinct herbal taste. Absinthe is traditionally green in color, although it can also be clear.

LIQUEURS

As you know, anything involving spirits is sure to make for a fun evening, whether that be alcohol or ghostly apparitions. Let's focus on the former and let the featured tales focus on the latter. Liqueurs are alcoholic drinks made from spirits flavored with all kinds of syrups, such as sugar, fruits, florals, or herbs. Discussed in the recipes in this book are liqueurs such as chocolate, elderflower (such as St-Germain), raspberry, schnapps, amaretto, blackberry, banana, coffee (such as Kahlúa), Irish cream (such as Bailey's), crème de cassis (such as DeKuyper), crème de menthe, crème de cacao, Scotch whisky liqueur (such as Drambuie), and maraschino.

Other liqueurs the book references are Italian red bitters to make a Negroni, with the most common brand used being Campari. The book also recommends a white wine–based aperitif, such as a Lillet Blanc. Brand names may be referenced to provide you with some ideas, but please follow your blackest of hearts toward the brands you feel best fit.

WINES

Many a ghastly story begins with a glass of wine. The term "wine" refers to alcoholic drinks made from fermented fruit juices, primarily grapes. This wretched recipe book will mention several types of wine such as brandy (a distilled wine), sherry (a fortified wine from Spain), cognac (a type of brandy distilled in France), vermouth (a fortified wine that has been flavored with herbs, can be sweet or dry), champagne (a sparkling white wine from its namesake region of France), and prosecco (a sparkling white wine from specific regions of Italy).

BEERS

Beers are fermented, alcoholic beverages made from malt and flavored with hops. Some of the recipes in this book call for pale ale (an amber-colored beer made from pale malt) or lager (another type of pale beer). Ginger beer is also mentioned in these recipes, which is a sweetened, carbonated drink with a strong ginger flavor, and is usually nonalcoholic.

OTHER POTIONS

Let's review some other potions suggested in these recipes. Bitters refer to alcoholic liquors flavored with bitter or aromatic botanicals. Some of the recipes may call for aromatic bitters with flavors specific to a recommended brand, such as Angostura or Peychaud. These recipes will suggest using these brands for their unique tastes, but if the spirits move you to a different aromatic bitter, heed the call as needed.

Syrups add delicious flavors to your cocktails. Most commonly used is a simple syrup, made from an equal amount of sugar and water. It is possible to make your own in a fairly simple concoction. Add your equal parts sugar and water to a saucepan over medium heat. Bring the combination to a simmer while stirring until the sugar is completely dissolved, approximately 2 to 3 minutes. Of course, it is also easy to purchase premade simple syrup from a variety of brands. Also recommended in this book are flavor-specific syrups such as grenadine (a pomegranate syrup), raspberry syrup, or agave syrup (a syrup derived from an agave plant).

Now that you know the basics, let's dive deep into the despair of the cocktail.

THE CLASSICS (1764–1970)

THE TURN OF THE SCREWDRIVER

The Turn of the Screw
by Henry James (1898)

Taking care of children is hard. Taking care of someone else's children is even harder. But taking care of someone's unwanted children on a haunted estate is impossible. You are always being compared with the person you replaced. Their marks can be seen everywhere. It's like they are following you around. How could anyone cope with these working conditions? The unnamed governess in this tale tries her best but still fails. She is hired by the children's uncle, who refuses to leave his London bachelor pad to raise his orphaned niece and nephew. Our governess must travel to his country estate and care for them despite it being a hostile work environment with a haunted work culture. Maybe a refreshing pop of citrus in her drink might have given her the strength and clarity to battle the ghosts haunting her wards, but alas those work perks were not there. Henry James tapped into his age's obsession with spiritualism to craft a chilling story of ghosts, class, love, and madness. This take on a screwdriver pays homage to the novella's English setting. Feel free to use vodka instead for a classic version of this cocktail.

YIELD: 1 serving

2 ounces gin

6 ounces orange juice

orange slice or twist, for garnish (optional)

1. Fill a highball glass with ice cubes.
2. Pour the gin over the ice.
3. Top with orange juice, filling to your desired level.
4. Stir gently to combine.
5. Garnish with an orange slice or twist, if using.
6. Serve immediately and enjoy responsibly!

CARMILLA CRIMSON COOLER

Carmilla
by Sheridan Le Fanu (1872)

Before *Dracula* swept into the world, there was *Carmilla*. Beautiful and mysterious, Carmilla slips into the life (and bed) of innocent protagonist Laura. Their intense connection is both dangerous and romantic, because Carmilla is—tragically—a blood-sucking vampire with an immortal history of murder and mayhem. As you indulge in your sanguine sip, take the time to wonder this: If Carmilla came to you on a moonless night, would you join her in her bloody crusade, or find a stake and be done with the drama?

Her soft cheek was glowing against mine. "Darling, darling," she murmured, "I live in you; and you would die for me, I love you so."

YIELD: 1 serving

2 ounces vodka (or gin if you prefer)

4 ounces cranberry juice

2 ounces grapefruit juice (preferably ruby red)

½ ounce freshly squeezed lime juice

soda water or club soda

lime wheel or twist, for garnish (optional)

fresh cranberries, for garnish (optional)

1. Fill a tall glass with ice cubes.
2. Pour the vodka, cranberry juice, grapefruit juice, and lime juice over the ice.
3. Stir gently to combine.
4. Top off with soda water or club soda, leaving about an inch from the rim.
5. Gently stir once more to integrate the soda.
6. Garnish with a lime wheel or twist and a few fresh cranberries, if using.

THE CASTLE OF OTRANTO OLD-FASHIONED

The Castle of Otranto
by Horace Walpole (1764)

The original gothic story, which kicked off an entire genre. Horace Walpole was inspired by ghostly nightmares he had at his spooky English mansion. The old-fashioned tale of Prince Manfred, who is driven mad after his son is killed on his wedding day by a giant falling helmet, is a timeless classic—just like this drink. The novel has all the elements that define the genre: paintings haunted by ghosts, forbidden lust, hidden royal identities, love triangles, chases through fantastical castles, and women threatened into nunhood. Manfred might have benefited from taking a break to enjoy one of these drinks and processing his emotions instead of desperately trying to force a divorce on his wife and attempting to marry his would-be daughter-in-law.

The hearts of both had drunk so deeply of a passion which both now tasted for the first time.

YIELD: 1 serving

1 sugar cube or ½ teaspoon granulated sugar

2 or 3 dashes Angostura bitters

2 ounces bourbon or rye whiskey

orange twist or slice, for garnish (optional)

maraschino cherry, for garnish (optional)

1. Place the sugar cube or granulated sugar in an old-fashioned glass and wet the sugar with the Angostura bitters.
2. Muddle the sugar and bitters until the sugar is dissolved.
3. Fill the glass with ice cubes or one large ice sphere.
4. Pour the bourbon or rye whiskey over the ice.
5. Stir gently to combine.
6. Garnish with an orange twist or slice and a maraschino cherry, if using.

THE WOMAN IN WHITE WINE SPRITZER

The Woman in White
by Wilkie Collins (1859)

The Woman in White is a complicated novel of switched identities, damsels in distress, wicked counts, and yes, a mysterious woman in white. As you puzzle your way through the tangled webs of the story, you may find yourself seeking a simple pleasure to pair with the perplexing plot. With just two ingredients, you can make a delicious foundation to dress up with your favorite garnishes. You'll already be shivering from the cool cruelty of men wrongfully imprisoning women in asylums, but be sure to keep your wine and soda as cold as possible for the best results.

YIELD: 1 serving

4 ounces white wine (such as sauvignon blanc or pinot grigio)

2 ounces soda water or club soda

lemon or lime wedge, for garnish (optional)

1. Fill a wine glass with ice cubes.
2. Pour the white wine into the glass.
3. Top the wine with soda water or club soda, adjusting the amount to your desired level of effervescence.
4. Gently stir to mix the wine and soda water or club soda.
5. Garnish with a lemon or lime wedge, if using.

FRANKEN-STEIN

Frankenstein; or, The Modern Prometheus
by Mary Shelley (1818)

A young Victor Frankenstein watches his mother die of scarlet fever before he heads off to university, where he buries himself in experiments and develops a way to impart life to nonliving matter. From his grief is born a monster. Victor swears to destroy his creation and embarks on a cat-and-mouse chase, ending in his own death and the monster drifting away into the Arctic on an ice raft. This dour yet thrilling meditation on humanity, morality, and death would pair well with something bright and citrusy to melt away the ice and, with any luck, deter you from reanimating any corpses.

All men hate the wretched; how then, must I be hated, who am miserable beyond all living things! Yet you, my creator, detest and spurn me, thy creature, to whom thou art bound by ties only dissoluble by the annihilation of one of us.

YIELD: 1 serving

6 ounces beer (lager or light beer works well)

6 ounces lemonade (store-bought or homemade)

lemon wedge, for garnish (optional)

1. Select a tall glass for your drink.
2. Pour the beer into the glass.
3. Pour the lemonade into the glass.
4. Adjust the ratio of beer to lemonade based on your preference for a stronger or weaker drink.
5. Give the shandy a gentle stir to combine the beer and lemonade.
6. Garnish the drink with a lemon wedge on the rim of the glass, if using.

THE PICTURE OF DORIAN GREY GOOSE

The Picture of Dorian Gray by Oscar Wilde (1891)

Handsome, hedonistic, and narcissistic, Dorian Gray wishes that his portrait would age instead of himself. Beauty above all else, am I right? This wish leads Dorian down a path of amorality, deceit, exploitation, and cruelty . . . you know, the fun stuff. His portrait takes all this abuse and becomes grotesque and unrecognizable. We sometimes think photos of ourselves look nothing like us—but this is intense. Redemption comes to Dorian only through destroying his own portrait and thus killing himself. Why not pair this Oscar Wilde classic with a decadent take on a martini? Indulge your vices.

YIELD: 1 serving

2 ounces vodka

¼ ounce dry vermouth

¼ ounce absinthe, for washing

blue cheese–stuffed olive, for garnish

1. Chill a martini glass by placing it in the freezer while you prepare the cocktail.
2. Fill a separate mixing glass with ice cubes to chill the vodka and dry vermouth.
3. Pour the vodka and dry vermouth into the ice-filled mixing glass. You can choose to stir or shake the mixture, depending on your preference.
4. Discard the ice from the mixing glass.
5. Pour the absinthe into the chilled martini glass. Coat the interior by swirling the glass, then discard the excess.
6. Strain the chilled vodka and dry vermouth mixture into the glass.
7. Skewer a blue cheese–stuffed olive on a cocktail pick, and place it in the martini as a garnish.

MANDERLEY MULE

Rebecca
by Daphne du Maurier (1938)

"Last night I dreamt I went to Manderley again." With that iconic first line, we jump into *Rebecca*, a story about an unnamed narrator who, after a whirlwind romance, marries a mysterious wealthy man and joins him at his grand estate known as Manderley. Followed closely by menacing housekeeper Mrs. Danvers, our narrator must navigate Manderley and the ever-present memory of her husband's first wife, Rebecca. As you walk the haunted halls of Manderley with the new Mrs. de Winter, toast to the macabre manor with a classic Moscow mule.

YIELD: 1 serving

2 ounces vodka

½ ounce freshly squeezed lime juice

ginger beer

lime wedge, for garnish

1. Fill a copper mug (or a highball glass) with ice cubes.
2. Pour the vodka and lime juice over the ice.
3. Top with the ginger beer, leaving some room for fizz.
4. Stir gently to mix the ingredients.
5. Garnish with the lime wedge.

Note: For a colorful twist to celebrate your escape from the clutches of the obsessive Mrs. Danvers, try adding a handful of fresh berries to the drink before stirring. Then muddle the berries as you stir, and top with some mint leaves. Ah, isn't it refreshing to be free from the constant comparison with a dead woman whose legacy you will never match, due to the very nature of memory and of death? Thank your lucky stars that you are no longer the new Mrs. de Winter!

WE ALWAYS HAVE COSMOS IN THE CASTLE

We Have Always Lived in the Castle
by Shirley Jackson (1962)

In Shirley Jackson's famous novel about family, community, rumors, and death, Merricat and Constance Blackwood are ostracized from their small town after Constance is accused of murdering much of the rest of their family. As hinted at in the rhyme created by the children in their town, arsenic replaced the sugar in its bowl. This was then dusted on top of a dessert of sweet blackberries. Let's take some inspiration from this dreadful deed and create a Blackwood-inspired cocktail—just be sure to keep the arsenic far from the blackberries in this instance.

Merricat, said Connie, would you like a cup of tea?
Oh no, said Merricat, you'll poison me.
Merricat, said Connie, would you like to go to sleep?
Down in the boneyard ten feet deep!

YIELD: 1 serving

6 to 8 fresh blackberries

2 ounces vodka

1 ounce triple sec or orange liqueur

1 ounce cranberry juice

½ ounce freshly squeezed lime juice

blackberries, for garnish

1. In a shaker, muddle the fresh blackberries to release their juices.
2. Add the vodka, triple sec or orange liqueur, cranberry juice, and lime juice to the shaker.
3. Fill the shaker with ice cubes.
4. Shake the ingredients well to chill the mixture.
5. Strain the cocktail into a chilled martini glass or a coupe glass.
6. Garnish with a few blackberries. If you'd like to add some sugar to them, then feel free—but be sure that what you sprinkle on top is indeed just sugar.

THE HAUNTING OF HIGHBALL HOUSE

The Haunting of Hill House
by Shirley Jackson (1959)

One of the most famous haunted house books in the genre, *The Haunting of Hill House* explores not only the unsettling interior of the titular Hill House but also the fragile psyche of protagonist Eleanor Vance. After taking the terrifying trip through Hill House, you may need a drink and a comforting hand to hold. But reader beware: sometimes the hand you're holding does not belong to the person you thought it did. In fact, it may not belong to a person at all. Lock your doors tight and try not to read the handwriting on the wall as you sip this spicy take on a classic highball.

No live organism can continue for long to exist sanely under conditions of absolute reality; even larks and katydids are supposed, by some, to dream. Hill House, not sane, stood by itself against its hills, holding darkness within; it had stood so for eighty years and might stand for eighty more. Within, walls continued upright, bricks met neatly, floors were firm, and doors were sensibly shut; silence lay steadily against the wood and stone of Hill House, and whatever walked there, walked alone.

YIELD: 1 serving

2 ounces whiskey (or the base spirit of your choice)

ginger beer or ginger ale, depending on your preferred spice level

lemon or lime wedge, for garnish

1. Fill a highball glass with ice cubes.
2. Pour the whiskey or the base spirit of your choice over the ice.
3. Top with the ginger beer or ginger ale, adjusting the amount to your desired level of spice.
4. Stir gently to mix the ingredients.
5. Garnish with the lemon or lime wedge.

A FROSÉ FOR EMILY

"A Rose for Emily"
by William Faulkner (1930)

In William Faulkner's Southern gothic short story "A Rose for Emily," the funeral of a reclusive elderly woman unburies some tragic secrets. While taking a stroll through her fictional Southern small town, you will find yourself wanting to enjoy a classic wine—but beware. After all, the titular Emily's stubborn resistance to change has some uniquely fatal consequences. Cool yourself with this frozen version of a favorite wine. Then perhaps change the pillowcases on your bed before resting. You wouldn't want an indentation of a head on the pillows to leave an implication that will haunt this oppressive small town. Then again, maybe you'd enjoy being a legend.

YIELD: 3 or 4 servings

1 (750 milliliter) bottle rosé

¼ cup sugar

¼ cup water

1 cup frozen strawberries

¼ cup freshly squeezed lemon juice

fresh berries or a lemon slice, for garnish (optional)

1. Pour the rosé into an ice cube tray and freeze until solid (at least 6 hours or overnight).
2. In a small saucepan, make a simple syrup by combining sugar and water over medium heat. Stir until the sugar dissolves. Allow the simple syrup to cool.
3. In a blender, combine the frozen rosé cubes, simple syrup, frozen strawberries, and lemon juice.
4. Blend the mixture until smooth and slushy.
5. Taste and adjust the sweetness by adding more simple syrup if needed.
6. Serve the frosé in glasses. Garnish with fresh berries or a lemon slice, if using.

The COUNT of MONTE CRISTAL

The Count of Monte Cristo
by Alexandre Dumas (1844)

Betrayal, prison breaks, treasure hunts, makeovers, revenge, and boats: this gargantuan novel has it all—and to think it's based on a true story. Alexandre Dumas's tale of Edmond Dantès's transformation from scorned sailor into the mysterious Count of Monte Cristo will make you question who your real friends are, and also make you wish you had used that one phone call at the police station to call your lawyer. Tracking down his betrayers and serving them a taste of their own medicine is monumental for Edmond, definitely worth popping a bottle of bubbly to celebrate. Let's pay homage to the Italian homeland of this "count" with an effervescent take on a classic Negroni to lift your spirits and deter you from carrying out your own revenge fantasy.

YIELD: 1 serving

1 ounce gin

1 ounce sweet vermouth

1 ounce Campari

1 ounce freshly squeezed grapefruit juice

about 2 ounces champagne or prosecco

orange twist or grapefruit slice, for garnish

1. Fill a mixing glass with ice cubes.
2. Pour the gin, sweet vermouth, Campari, and grapefruit juice into the mixing glass.
3. Stir the ingredients well for 30 seconds in order to chill the mixture.
4. Strain the mixture from the mixing glass into an ice-filled rocks glass.
5. Pour the champagne or prosecco into the glass, allowing it to mix with the other ingredients.
6. Garnish with the orange twist or grapefruit slice.

ROSEMARY'S BAILEYS

Rosemary's Baby
by Ira Levin (1967)

Motherhood can be a devil. In Ira Levin's iconic novel *Rosemary's Baby*, Rosemary Woodhouse must juggle her smarmy husband, Guy, her nosy neighbors, and a pregnancy from hell. *Rosemary's Baby* highlights the horror of being a woman disbelieved by her community while being taken advantage of at her most vulnerable. If anyone deserves a delicious respite in the midst of caring for a young demon, it's Rosemary.

YIELD: 1 serving

1 ounce coffee liqueur (for example, Kahlúa)

1 ounce Irish cream liqueur (for example, Baileys)

1 ounce amaretto

1 ounce vodka

1 ounce heavy cream

1. Fill a shaker with ice cubes.
2. Add the coffee liqueur, Irish cream, amaretto, vodka, and heavy cream to the shaker.
3. Shake the ingredients well to chill the mixture.
4. Strain the cocktail into an ice-filled rocks glass.

ANNABELLINI LEE

"Annabel Lee"
by Edgar Allan Poe (1849)

The final finished poem by Edgar Allan Poe chronicles the tragic story of a young man and woman so desperately in love that the angels became jealous. The young man narrates the story of their everlasting love in their kingdom by the sea. After the untimely death of the maiden Annabel Lee, their connection remains so intense that the narrator sleeps every night next to her tomb. Yikes. A night near the tombs cannot be very restful, so treat yourself to a sweet cocktail. Peaches and champagne make up this delightful brew, something sweet to console you—as you look out across the sounding sea and mourn the beautiful, beautiful Annabel Lee.

YIELD: 1 serving

2 ounces peach puree (fresh or store-bought)

4 ounces prosecco (chilled)

peach slice or raspberry, for garnish (optional)

1. If you are using fresh peaches, then peel and pit them. Blend the peaches until you have a smooth puree.
2. Spoon the peach puree into a chilled champagne flute.
3. Top the peach puree with chilled prosecco, filling the glass.
4. Stir gently to mix the ingredients.
5. Garnish with a peach slice or a raspberry, if using.

THE TELL-TALE TART

"The Tell-Tale Heart"
by Edgar Allan Poe (1843)

Do you hear that? In Edgar Allan Poe's timeless tale of murder and guilt, the paranoid narrator kills and dismembers an elderly man and hides his body beneath the floorboards. The narrator is driven to confession after hearing the persistent beating of the dead man's heart. A tale this bitter deserves a drink that's intensely tart. Try this sour cocktail and don't forget to top it off with a heart-shaped garnish, just so you don't forget what you've done. Do you hear it now?

YIELD: 1 serving

2 ounces gin

¾ ounce freshly squeezed lemon juice

½ ounce simple syrup (adjust to taste)

lemon peel, for garnish

1. In a shaker, combine the gin, lemon juice, and simple syrup.
2. Add ice cubes to the shaker.
3. Shake the ingredients well to chill the mixture.
4. Strain the cocktail into a rocks glass filled with ice.
5. Fold a thin strip of lemon peel into the shape of a heart, and pierce it with a toothpick to keep its shape.

THE RAVEN RUM RUNNER

"The Raven"
by Edgar Allan Poe (1845)

Doesn't everyone want a bird companion to hang out with? And one that talks! That'd be the dream. Unless you are the narrator of "The Raven," who is despondent with grief over his lost Lenore. And it probably doesn't help that the raven in question can only say, "Nevermore." Hardly the kind of reinforcement you want from a friend. This aptly named cocktail should inspire you to do what the narrator of this poem does not do: run, run far away from that cursed bird.

Take thy beak from out my heart, and take thy form from off my door!
Quoth the Raven "Nevermore."

YIELD: 1 serving

1 ounce dark rum

1 ounce light rum

½ ounce crème de banana liqueur

½ ounce blackberry liqueur

1 ounce pineapple juice

1 ounce orange juice

½ ounce grenadine

maraschino cherry and orange slice, for garnish

1. Choose a hurricane glass or any large, tall glass. Fill it with crushed ice to create a refreshing base for your cocktail.
2. In a shaker, combine the dark and light rums.
3. Add the crème de banana liqueur and blackberry liqueur to the shaker.
4. Pour the pineapple juice and orange juice into the shaker.
5. Add the grenadine to the mix.
6. Shake the ingredients vigorously for about 10 to 15 seconds to ensure proper mixing and chilling.
7. Strain the mixture from the shaker into the prepared glass over the crushed ice.
8. Garnish with a maraschino cherry and an orange slice.

A STREET SIDECAR NAMED DESIRE

A Streetcar Named Desire
by Tennessee Williams (1947)

Blanche DuBois is down on her luck. She is a recent widow with a shadowed past who goes to live in New Orleans with her sister, Stella, and her brother-in-law, Stanley. We are witness to Blanche's slow descent into torpor through the machinations of Stanley—his manipulative abuse and inane screams of "Stella!" This classic Southern gothic play by Tennessee Williams can be paired with this famous cocktail so that you won't have to depend on the kindness of strangers to calm your nerves during these dramatic events.

YIELD: 1 serving

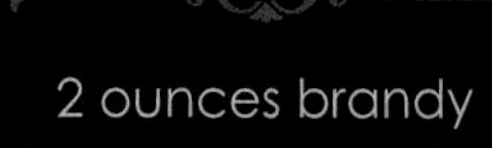

2 ounces brandy (cognac or another quality brandy)

¾ ounce triple sec

¾ ounce freshly squeezed lemon juice

½ ounce simple syrup (optional, adjust to taste)

sugar and lemon wedge, for rimming the glass (optional)

lemon twist, for garnish

1. If desired, moisten the rim with a lemon wedge, and then dip it into sugar to coat.
2. Fill a cocktail shaker with ice cubes.
3. Pour the brandy, triple sec, lemon juice, and simple syrup (adjust to taste) into the shaker.
4. Shake the ingredients vigorously for about 10 to 15 seconds.
5. Strain the contents into the prepared cocktail glass without ice.
6. Garnish with the lemon twist.

THE LEGEND OF SLUSHY HOLLOW

"The Legend of Sleepy Hollow" by Washington Irving (1820)

An essential entry into the canon of American horror, this short story details the trials and tribulations of the superstitious Ichabod Crane. Consider the delightful autumn ambiance of harvest parties, ghost stories, and a terrifying specter with a severed head. If this isn't enough to send shivers down your spine, then try this frosty take on grog.

YIELD: 1 serving

2 ounces dark rum

1 ounce water

½ ounce freshly squeezed lime juice

½ ounce honey or simple syrup

1. Combine water, dark rum, lime juice and honey or simple syrup in a blender. Add a generous amount of ice cubes to the blender.
2. Blend the ingredients until you achieve a slushy consistency. Add more ice if needed to reach the desired texture.
3. Pour the slushy grog into a glass.

GORMEN GRASSHOPPER

Titus Groan (1946), *Gormenghast* (1950), and *Titus Alone* (1959) by Mervyn Peake

Castle Gormenghast stands before you, a massive island of stone, home to the ancient noble ruling family Groan and their violet-eyed heir, Titus. This fantastical gothic series follows young Titus as he is reared in the labyrinthine castle. As Titus grows, an ambitious young kitchen boy named Steerpike schemes to find a way out of his menial life and into a position of power. This macabre series deserves a sweet cocktail to offset the horrors that reside within the castle.

And now, my poor old woman, why are you crying so bitterly? It is autumn. The leaves are falling from the trees like burning tears—the wind howls. Why must you mimic them?

YIELD: 1 serving

¾ ounce white crème de cacao

¾ ounce green crème de menthe

¾ ounce cream

fresh mint leaves, for garnish (optional)

1. Fill a cocktail shaker with ice cubes.
2. Pour the white crème de cacao, green crème de menthe, and cream into the shaker.
3. Shake the ingredients vigorously for about 10 to 15 seconds.
4. Strain the mixture from the shaker into a chilled cocktail glass (you can use a martini glass or a coupe glass).
5. Garnish with fresh mint leaves, if using.

CAT ON A HOT GIN ROOF

Cat on a Hot Tin Roof by Tennessee Williams (1955)

Tennessee Williams is a master of the Southern gothic drama, and this play is one of his most celebrated. It follows the Pollitt family during one night of celebrating the return of Big Daddy from the hospital with what everyone thinks is good news. Lies, deceit, betrayal, and death abound in the course of this raucous night in Mississippi. Heat up this twist on a classic cocktail, and hope that your family doesn't lie to you about a terminal illness.

YIELD: 1 serving

2 ounces gin

1 cup water

1 cinnamon stick

3 whole cloves

1 tablespoon honey

½ ounce freshly squeezed lemon juice

lemon slice, for garnish

1. Pour the gin into a mug or heatproof glass.
2. Pour the water into a saucepan. Add the cinnamon stick, cloves, honey, and lemon juice.
3. Heat gently over a low heat until simmering.
4. Strain the mixture and pour into the mug or heatproof glass.
5. Stir the mixture gently to combine.
6. Garnish with the lemon slice.

A GOOD MANHATTAN IS HARD TO FIND

"A Good Man Is Hard to Find"
by Flannery O'Connor (1953)

Considered a trailblazer in the genre of Southern gothic fiction, Flannery O'Connor's most famous work follows a Southern family who encounter a trio of criminals led by the escaped convict The Misfit when leaving for vacation. As you read this story of despair and grace, try to find a moment of peace with a sip of this delicious cocktail.

YIELD: 1 serving

2 ounces rye whiskey or bourbon

1 ounce sweet vermouth

2 or 3 dashes Angostura bitters

maraschino cherry or twist of orange peel, for garnish

1. Fill a mixing glass with ice cubes.
2. Pour the rye whiskey or bourbon, sweet vermouth, and Angostura bitters into the mixing glass.
3. Stir the ingredients well for about 15 to 20 seconds to chill the mixture.
4. Strain the cocktail into a chilled martini or rocks glass.
5. Garnish with the maraschino cherry or twist of orange peel. To create an orange twist, express the oils from a thin strip of orange peel over the drink, and then drop the orange peel into the glass.

TRANSYLVANIA TERMINATOR

Dracula
by Bram Stoker (1897)

Told through letters and journal entries, the quintessential vampire tale begins with Jonathan Harker bumbling through the Transylvanian countryside before running into one of the most famous villains of all time—the terrifying Dracula. This iconic vampire tale is chock-full of twists, turns, and horrors, and it features what may be the scariest ship voyage ever. Think of the heroic Van Helsing battling Dracula while you sip this terrifying cocktail.

YIELD: 1 serving

1 ounce coffee liqueur (for example, Kahlúa)

1 ounce Irish cream liqueur (for example, Baileys)

1 ounce dark rum

1 ounce vodka

½ ounce simple syrup

1. Choose a rocks glass or a short tumbler, and fill it with ice cubes to chill the glass.
2. Pour the coffee liqueur over the ice in the glass.
3. Add the Irish cream liqueur to the glass.
4. Pour the dark rum and the vodka into the glass.
5. Add the simple syrup to the mix. Adjust the sweetness according to your preference.
6. Gently stir the ingredients in the glass to ensure that they are well combined.

JANE EYRE ROYALE

Jane Eyre
by Charlotte Brontë (1847)

Jane Eyre had some tough times. First she lived at Gateshead Hall with her abusive aunt and uncle. Then she was shipped off to the Lockwood Institution, where she encountered even more abuse. Finally, Jane got a seeming reprieve when she secured work as the governess of Thornfield and fell in love with Edward Rochester, the master of the house. Of course, all was not as it seemed: Thornfield Hall had secrets and so did Mr. Rochester. If only Jane had had a friend to whip up some Kir Royales and suggest that they check out those noises coming from the spooky attic.

YIELD: 1 serving

½ ounce crème de cassis (black currant liqueur)

5 ounces chilled champagne or sparkling wine

fresh black currants or a lemon twist, for garnish (optional)

1. Pour the crème de cassis into a champagne flute.
2. Carefully pour the chilled champagne or sparkling wine over the crème de cassis.
3. Garnish with a few fresh black currants or a lemon twist, if using.

A DARK AND STORMY NIGHT IN THE HOUSE OF USHER

"The Fall of the House of Usher"
by Edgar Allan Poe (1839)

Have you ever walked into an uncomfortable family dynamic at a friend's house in which you do not have the full context but you know there is a deep dysfunction at play? This is the plight of the narrator of one of Poe's most gothic stories, "The Fall of the House of Usher." The narrator witnesses some truly unsettling sibling moments as he tries to make the best of the evening. Unfortunately for all involved, the stormy sip will not be a pleasant one. Ease the narrator's discomfort with a classic cocktail with a fitting name.

YIELD: 1 serving

2 ounces dark rum

½ ounce freshly squeezed lime juice (juiced from half of a lime)

3 ounces ginger beer

lime wedge, for garnish

1. Take a highball glass and fill it with ice cubes.
2. Pour the dark rum over the ice.
3. Squeeze lime juice into the glass.
4. Pour the ginger beer over the rum and lime juice.
5. Gently stir the drink. Be careful not to overstir, as it will muddy the layers of your drink. You don't want to cause restless spirits, after all.
6. Garnish with the lime wedge.

SOUR STONING

The Lottery

by Shirley Jackson (1948)

Imagine: It's June 27 and it's time for your village's annual lottery, a tradition that ensures a good harvest for the coming fall. Some villages nearby have discontinued their lotteries, but your village knows that it's a time-honored and valued custom. In fact, your village is so devoted to the tradition that its residents refuse to replace the rather decrepit lottery box! Many things have changed since the beginning, but the residents still remember to use stones. Before it's your turn to draw your slip of paper, sip this citrusy take on a whiskey sour.

YIELD: 1 serving

2 ounces bourbon

1 ounce orange juice

¾ ounce freshly squeezed lemon juice

½ ounce simple syrup (adjust to taste)

orange slice, for garnish

1. Fill a rocks glass with ice cubes.
2. In a shaker, add the bourbon, orange juice, lemon juice, and simple syrup.
3. Shake the ingredients for about 10 to 15 seconds to ensure that they are thoroughly mixed and chilled.
4. Strain the mixture into the ice-filled rocks glass.
5. Garnish the drink with the orange slice.

WUTHERING FLIGHTS

Wuthering Heights
by Emily Brontë (1847)

Is there a romance more classically gothic than *Wuthering Heights*? In Emily Brontë's windswept novel, doomed lovers Heathcliff and Catherine rage against their circumstances, the moors, and each other. Ghosts may or may not stalk the grounds, and the inhabitants—and readers—are left haunted. Invite some friends to wallow and perhaps play the Kate Bush song of the same name. Together, you can take some small but dark-and-stormy-inspired sweet shots in honor of this dark and stormy relationship.

YIELD: 4 servings (4 shots)

4 ounces dark rum

2 ounces ginger beer

1 ounce freshly squeezed lime juice

1 ounce simple syrup

1. Gather the dark rum, ginger beer, lime juice, and simple syrup.
2. In a cocktail shaker, combine the ingredients.
3. Shake the ingredients in the shaker for about 10 to 15 seconds to ensure that they are thoroughly mixed and chilled.
4. Strain the mixture into shot glasses.

THE HEART IS A LONELY MIXER

The Heart Is a Lonely Hunter
by Carson McCullers (1940)

Loneliness abounds in this dreary Southern gothic tale. John Singer, a deaf man, encounters several people in a Georgia mill town. They all gravitate toward Singer and his generosity in meeting their needs. But they are all ultimately stymied in their pursuits through circumstances outside anyone's control. Pair the bleak, isolating world of Singer with an equally lonely-feeling cocktail, which has only two ingredients

YIELD: 1 serving

2 ounces Scotch whisky

½ ounce Drambuie

lemon twist, for garnish

1. Fill a mixing glass with ice cubes.
2. Pour your preferred Scotch whisky into the mixing glass.
3. Add the Drambuie to the Scotch in the mixing glass.
4. Stir the mixture well using a bar spoon or mixing stick.
5. Strain the mixture from the mixing glass into an ice-filled rocks glass.
6. Garnish with the lemon twist.

THE PHANTOM COLLINS OF THE OPERA

The Phantom of the Opera
by Gaston Leroux (1909)

Can you hear it, the music of the night? In 1880s Paris, the grand Palais Garnier opera house is plagued by rumors of an apparition haunting its halls. As chandeliers fall and ingenues are abducted, unwind with a grand operatic soundtrack and a classy drink. Take a sip and imagine yourself in the dank depths of an operatic lair, and be prepared to unmask a phantom.

Know that it is a corpse who loves you and adores you and will never, never leave you!

YIELD: 1 serving

2 ounces gin

¾ ounce simple syrup

1 ounce freshly squeezed lemon juice

soda water or club soda

lemon slice and cherry, for garnish

1. Fill a Collins glass with ice cubes to chill it.
2. Pour the gin over the ice.
3. Add the simple syrup to the glass. You can adjust the sweetness based on your preference.
4. Add the lemon juice to the glass.
5. Stir the ingredients well to ensure that they are thoroughly mixed.
6. Top up the glass with soda water or club soda to your desired level. The amount may vary, but it's typically around 2 to 3 ounces.
7. Add a lemon slice to the rim of the glass, and let a cherry float on top of the drink.

THE STRANGE CASE OF DR. JEKYLL AND MUDSLIDE

The Strange Case of Dr. Jekyll and Mr. Hyde
by Robert Louis Stevenson (1886)

The duality of humans is a common trope in gothic literature, and one devilishly explored by Robert Louis Stevenson in this classic tale of a man and his inner vices battling for control. Dr. Jekyll slowly loses power over Mr. Hyde, who grows stronger with each transformation while his list of crimes grows longer. Indulge your inner vices with this decadent chocolaty treat of a cocktail, and hope it doesn't lead to any monstrous transmogrifications.

YIELD: 1 serving

1 ounce vodka

1 ounce coffee liqueur (for example, Kahlúa)

1 ounce Irish cream liqueur (for example, Baileys)

chocolate syrup

whipped cream, for garnish (optional)

1. Add the vodka, coffee liqueur, and Irish cream liqueur to a mixing glass.
2. Fill the mixing glass with ice cubes.
3. Choose a rocks glass or a short tumbler, and drizzle chocolate syrup along the inside of the glass.
4. Strain the mixture of vodka and liqueurs into the prepared glass.
5. Garnish with a dollop of whipped cream, if using.

AS I LAY DRYING

As I Lay Dying
by William Faulkner (1930)

What is objective truth? Does it even exist? What better way to explore it than a dour tale of a family's journey with the unembalmed body of their matriarch to her hometown to bury her. Dizzyingly told through multiple family members' perspectives, this Southern gothic novel grapples with the nature of existence. The family's grim trek offers little levity, so why not pair this story with a dry martini to jump straight to the punch.

YIELD: 1 serving

2 ounces gin

½ ounce dry vermouth

olive or lemon twist, for garnish

1. Fill a mixing glass with ice cubes.
2. Pour the gin into the mixing glass.
3. Add the dry vermouth to the gin.
4. Stir the ingredients in the mixing glass gently but thoroughly for about 15 to 20 seconds.
5. Strain the contents of the mixing glass into a chilled martini glass.
6. Garnish with an olive or a lemon twist.

THE MEZCALS OF UDOLPHO

The Mysteries of Udolpho
by Ann Radcliffe (1794)

This early text of gothic literature follows the tragedies and romances of Emily St. Aubert as she travels through Europe, becomes an orphan, falls in love with a sensitive man, and is imprisoned by the devious Signor Montoni in the eponymous Castle Udolpho. Despair and death overflow the pages of this book and threaten to drown Emily, but she perseveres with tenacity. Experience the dank halls of the castle with this warm, bright cocktail to cheer you.

YIELD: 1 serving

2 ounces mezcal

1 ounce triple sec or orange liqueur

¾ ounce freshly squeezed lime juice

½ ounce agave syrup (adjust to taste)

salt and lime wedge, for rimming the glass (optional)

lime wheel, for garnish

1. Fill a cocktail shaker with ice cubes to chill the ingredients.
2. Pour the mezcal and triple sec or orange liqueur into the shaker.
3. Add the lime juice to the shaker.
4. Pour the agave syrup into the shaker.
5. Shake the ingredients vigorously for about 10 to 15 seconds.
6. If desired, rim a rocks glass with salt. To do this, moisten the rim with a lime wedge and dip it into salt to coat.
7. Strain the contents of the shaker into the prepared rocks glass filled with ice.
8. Garnish with the lime wheel.

A CHRISTMAS CAÇHAÇA

A Christmas Carol
by Charles Dickens (1843)

This Christmas classic, brimming with gothic delights, set many of the holiday traditions still around today. Scarily enough, it also set many of our spooky standards as well. The miserly Scrooge is haunted by the Ghosts of Christmas Past, Present, and Yet to Come, who take him on a terrifying, transformative journey. Mix up this holiday spin on a tropical favorite, and see if a vile wretch can find redemption.

YIELD: 1 serving

4 to 6 fresh cranberries

2 ounces cachaça

1 ounce cranberry juice

½ ounce simple syrup

½ ounce freshly squeezed lime juice, from half of a lime

rosemary sprig, for garnish

1. In a shaker, muddle the fresh cranberries to release their juices.
2. Pour the cachaça into the shaker.
3. Add the cranberry juice and simple syrup to the mix.
4. Squeeze lime juice into the shaker.
5. Shake the ingredients vigorously for about 10 to 15 seconds.
6. Strain the cocktail into a rocks glass or a festive glass filled with ice.
7. Garnish with the rosemary sprig.

THE GREYHOUND OF THE BASKERVILLES

The Hound of the Baskervilles
by Sir Arthur Conan Doyle (1902)

Widely considered one of the best Sherlock Holmes novels by fans and critics alike, this story features a demonic hound stalking the foggy moors of Baskerville Hall. When Sherlock and his bestie Dr. Watson arrive to solve the mystery of the murderous hound, they uncover family secrets and sinister plans. As you follow the dynamic duo through the dreary landscape and deadly plots, enjoy a sophisticated sip of this simple cocktail.

It came with the wind through the silence of the night, a long, deep mutter, then a rising howl, and then the sad moan in which it died away. Again and again it sounded, the whole air throbbing with it, strident, wild and menacing.

YIELD: 1 serving

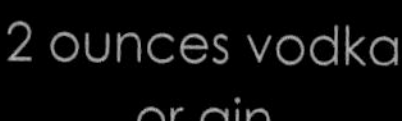

2 ounces vodka or gin

5 ounces grapefruit juice (freshly squeezed if possible)

salt and grapefruit wedge, for rimming the glass (optional)

grapefruit slice or wedge, for garnish (optional)

1. If you like, you can rim the glass with salt. To do this, moisten the rim with a grapefruit wedge. Then dip the grapefruit wedge into a plate of salt. Coat the rim with this damp salt. This step is optional and depends on personal preference.
2. Fill a highball glass with ice cubes.
3. Pour the vodka or gin over the ice in the glass.
4. Top with the grapefruit juice.
5. Stir gently to mix the ingredients.
6. Garnish with a grapefruit slice or wedge, if using.

THE MOCK

The Monk
by Matthew Lewis (1796)

Hidden identities, demons, ghosts, fires, poison, exorcisms, and some racy scenes involving monks and nuns betraying their vows. All these, and truly so much more, are wrapped into this early gothic text. So much happens that it makes a mockery of your mind when you try to keep up with it all. Best to pair this horrifying tale with an enticing caffeinated mocktail so that you can keep your wits about you and avoid selling your soul to the devil.

YIELD: 1 serving

1 cup cola

½ ounce grenadine syrup

maraschino cherry, for garnish

1. Fill a highball glass with ice cubes.
2. Pour the cola into the glass.
3. Add the grenadine syrup to the cola.
4. Stir the ingredients gently to mix the grenadine into the cola slightly.
5. Garnish by dropping a maraschino cherry into the glass.

THE MODERN (1970–2022)

THE SLOE, SLOE WOODS

The Low, Low Woods
by Carmen Maria Machado (2020)

You and your friend wake up in a movie theater. Neither of you has any memory of the past few hours. You shudder to think what has happened. But wait, that's the name of the town you live in. Shudder-to-Think, Pennsylvania, is home to many dreadful things: rabbits with human eyes, skinless men, a deer woman who hunts hungry girls—and oh, the town has also been on fire for years. Should you and your friend try to get to the bottom of all these strange occurrences? Or just continue with your lives? Best to take things slow as you read this haunting graphic novel and sip on this classic drink.

YIELD: 1 serving

2 ounces sloe gin

¾ ounce freshly squeezed lemon juice

½ ounce simple syrup

soda water or club soda

lemon slice or twist, for garnish

1. Add ice cubes to a cocktail shaker.
2. Add the lemon juice, simple syrup, and sloe gin into the shaker.
3. Shake the ingredients vigorously for about 15 to 20 seconds.
4. Strain the contents of the shaker into a highball or Collins glass filled with ice.
5. Top with soda water or club soda, filling the glass to your desired level.
6. Garnish with the lemon slice or twist.

THE HOUSE ON VESPER MARTINI

The House on Vesper Sands
by Paraic O'Donnell (2018)

Brimming with wit, humor, and supernatural delights, this tale set in Victorian London offers some levity to a typically grim genre. Following a mysterious suicide, before which a cryptic message was sewed into the skin of the deceased, a team of unlikely sleuths tries to untangle events. Mix up a vibrant cocktail to help you guess who the culprit is.

YIELD: 1 serving

3 ounces London dry gin

1 ounce vodka

½ ounce Lillet Blanc (or Cocchi Americano)

lemon twist, for garnish

1. Place your martini glass in the freezer to chill.
2. Add ice cubes to a mixing glass.
3. Pour the London dry gin, vodka, and Lillet Blanc or Cocchi Americano into the mixing glass.
4. Stir the ingredients in the mixing glass using a bar spoon or stirring stick.
5. Remove the ice from the mixing glass, then strain the mixture from the mixing glass into the chilled martini glass.
6. Drop the lemon twist into the drink or garnish the martini glass with it.

TEQUILA IS THE FLESH

Tender Is the Flesh
by Agustina Bazterrica (2017)

Marcos is a purveyor of a special type of meat that is coveted worldwide. His father is dying, his son is dead, and he's separated from his wife and has now started an affair with a woman from work. None of this sounds too sinister, but once you know that this all takes place in a dystopian future in which cannibalism is normalized, and that the woman Marcos is having an affair with was bred to be slaughtered, you might think otherwise. Pair this wallop of a story with a drink that packs an equal punch.

YIELD: 1 serving

2 ounces blanco tequila

½ ounce freshly squeezed lime juice (juiced from half of a lime)

½ ounce simple syrup (optional, adjust to taste)

grapefruit soda

salt and lime wedge, for rimming the glass (optional)

grapefruit wedge, for garnish

1. Moisten the rim with a lime wedge. Then dip the lime wedge into salt and coat the rim with this damp salt.
2. Fill the prepared glass with ice cubes.
3. Pour the blanco tequila over the ice.
4. Squeeze the lime juice into the glass. Adjust the amount of lime juice to your taste preferences.
5. Add the simple syrup, if using. Adjust the sweetness to your liking.
6. Fill the glass with grapefruit soda, leaving about an inch of space at the top. You can adjust the ratio of tequila to soda based on your preference.
7. Gently stir the ingredients in the glass to combine the flavors.
8. Garnish with the grapefruit wedge on the rim for an extra citrusy touch.

WHAT REVIVES THE DEAD

What Moves the Dead
by T. Kingfisher (2022)

A moldering mansion near a menacing tarn with fields full of oddly behaving hares. This frightening setting is home to an imaginative and horrifying retelling of "The Fall of the House of Usher" by Edgar Allen Poe, which introduces a new mycological villain to the story. Madeleine Usher is host to a fungal invasion, which makes it appear that she is possessed. After she presumably dies, she is reanimated by her parasite to try to infect others. The Ushers' ancestral home falls in hopes of stopping the spread of this plague. This haunting update on a classic calls for a classic of its own, a Corpse Reviver, which with any luck won't get laced with a parasitic fungus.

YIELD: 1 serving

¾ ounce gin

¾ ounce Lillet Blanc (or Cocchi Americano)

¾ ounce orange liqueur

¾ ounce freshly squeezed lemon juice

1 dash absinthe (or absinthe substitute)

orange twist, for garnish

1. Fill a cocktail shaker with ice cubes to chill the ingredients.
2. Pour the gin, Lillet Blanc or Cocchi Americano, and orange liqueur into the shaker.
3. Add the lemon juice to the shaker.
4. Add a dash of absinthe or absinthe substitute to the shaker.
5. Shake the ingredients vigorously for about 10 to 15 seconds.
6. Strain the contents of the shaker into a chilled coupe glass or martini glass.
7. Garnish with the orange twist.

BLOODY MARY-IDIAN

Blood Meridian
by Cormac McCarthy (1985)

A book in the anti-western genre, this nihilistic and bloody novel takes place on the American frontier. As the reader follows a protagonist known as "the kid," a tale of bloodshed and violence unfolds to reveal the horrors of the early Americas. After such a bleak trip through time, reward yourself with a modern twist on a classic drink to ease the pain

YIELD: 1 serving

1½ ounces vodka

3 ounces tomato juice

½ ounce freshly squeezed lemon juice

1 dash Worcestershire sauce

1 dash hot sauce (adjust to taste)

celery salt and black pepper, to taste

celery stalk, lemon wedge, and olives, for garnish

1. Fill a shaker with ice cubes.
2. Add the vodka, tomato juice, lemon juice, Worcestershire sauce, hot sauce, celery salt, and black pepper to the shaker.
3. Shake the ingredients well to combine and chill.
4. Strain the mixture into an ice-filled highball glass.
5. Garnish with the celery stalk, lemon wedge, and olives.

RED RUM

The Shining
by Stephen King (1977)

Haunted houses are a classic trope in gothic literature, but what if, and this is gonna sound crazy, there were a haunted hotel . . . with all those rooms just brimming with psychic terror. Frightening! Unluckily for Jack Torrance and his family, who are hired to be the off-season caretakers of the Overlook Hotel in the Rockies, their new home is just that. Cabin fever sets in, and ghostly children, forbidden rooms, and animated topiaries topple the Torrance family. Sip on this fruity cocktail to warm your soul as you read this frigid tale.

YIELD: 1 serving

2 ounces light rum

½ ounce raspberry syrup (store-bought raspberry syrup or make your own by combining equal parts sugar, water, and fresh raspberries)

½ ounce curaçao

¾ ounce freshly squeezed lime juice (juiced from 1 lime)

orange slice or twist, for garnish

raspberry or cherry, for garnish

1. Add ice cubes to a cocktail shaker to chill the ingredients.
2. Add the light rum, raspberry syrup, and curaçao into the shaker.
3. Squeeze lime juice into the shaker.
4. Shake the ingredients vigorously for about 10 to 15 seconds.
5. Strain the contents of the shaker into a rocks glass or a coupe glass filled with ice.
6. Garnish with the orange slice or twist on the rim of the glass and the raspberry or cherry on top of the drink.

WET AND WYLDING HALL

Wylding Hall
by Elizabeth Hand (2015)

Let's go back to the 1970s with the fictional acid-folk band Windhollow Faire as they attempt to record their new album at the crumbling country house Wylding Hall. Things do not go as planned. If you're ready for a slow-creeping dread that crawls up your spine, then settle in with this novella and a delicious drink.

YIELD: 1 serving

½ ounce rum

1 ounce triple sec

1 ounce melon liqueur

½ ounce crème de almond

orange juice

orange slice, for garnish (optional)

1. Fill a highball or Collins glass with ice cubes.
2. Pour the rum, triple sec, melon liqueur, crème de almond, and orange juice over the ice.
3. Stir the ingredients to ensure that they are thoroughly mixed.
4. Garnish with an orange slice, if using.

THE GHOST IN THE GRAVEYARD BOOK

The Graveyard Book
by Neil Gaiman (2008)

Surprisingly, this neo-gothic tale about Nobody "Bod" Owens, whose family is brutally murdered and who is raised by supernatural guardians in a cemetery, is a children's book. Hiding from the ominous-sounding, and actually murderous, Jacks of All Trades, Bod must learn the ins and outs of living in a cemetery and also growing up—from escaping ghoul gates and ancient burial mounds to the first twinges of a young crush—all while minding his adoptive ghost parents. Mix up one of these ghostly libations to either wash away the troubles of parenthood or celebrate your lack of parental responsibilities.

It's only death. I mean, all of my best friends are dead.

YIELD: 1 serving

1½ ounces black vodka

1 ounce coffee liqueur (for example, Kahlúa)

½ ounce crème de cacao

2 ounces milk or cream

1. Fill a highball or rocks glass with crushed ice.
2. Pour the black vodka over the ice.
3. Pour the coffee liqueur over the black vodka.
4. Add the crème de cacao to the mix.
5. Pour the milk or cream over the other ingredients.
6. If you want a more uniform look, then gently stir the ingredients.

THE SOTOL HISTORY

The Secret History
by Donna Tartt (1992)

College is a time for most people to sow their wild oats, but for Richard Papen, it was a time for him to get embroiled in a bacchanalian murder cover-up. Set at an idyllic fictitious college in Vermont, this novel follows a group of classics students and their internal feuds and romances. Enjoy this cocktail while thinking back on your youthful years, which—knock on wood—unlike Richard's, weren't tinged with murder.

YIELD: 1 serving

2 ounces sotol (or blanco tequila if you can't find sotol)

1 ounce freshly squeezed lime juice

¾ ounce agave syrup (1:1 ratio of agave nectar to water)

½ ounce orange liqueur (for example, triple sec or Grand Marnier)

lime wheel, for garnish

1. Fill a cocktail shaker with ice cubes.
2. Add the sotol or blanco tequila, lime juice, agave syrup, and orange liqueur to the shaker.
3. Shake the ingredients vigorously for about 10 to 15 seconds.
4. Strain the contents of the shaker into a rocks glass filled with ice. You can also use a double rocks glass or a tumbler.
5. Garnish with the lime wheel.

CHAMPERS OF THE WIND

The Shadow of the Wind
by Carlos Ruiz Zafón (2001)

Daniel loves books, and his father takes him to the Cemetery of Forgotten Books, where he finds a book called *The Shadow of the Wind*—but wait, that's the name of the book you're reading. Daniel loves the book and wants to unravel the mystery of why he has the only copy in existence. Forbidden love abounds in this haunting tale, set in the aftermath of the Spanish Civil War. Sip on this bubbly Spanish cocktail while you and Daniel try to unravel the mystery.

A secret's worth depends on the people from whom it must be kept.

YIELD: 1 serving

1 ounce vodka

1 ounce gin

3 ounces freshly squeezed orange juice

½ ounce simple syrup (adjust amount to taste)

cava (Spanish sparkling wine), chilled

orange slice or twist, for garnish

1. Choose a large wine glass or a stemmed glass. Fill it with ice cubes to chill the glass.
2. Pour the vodka and gin into the glass.
3. Squeeze the orange juice.
4. Pour the orange juice into the glass with the vodka and gin.
5. Add the simple syrup to the mix. (Adjust the sweetness to your liking by adding more or less simple syrup.)
6. Gently stir the ingredients in the glass to combine and chill the mixture.
7. Fill the remainder of the glass with the chilled cava.
8. Garnish with the orange slice or twist.

HOUSE PARTY OF LEAVES

House of Leaves
by Mark Z. Danielewski (2000)

Let's have a house party! Take a drink and welcome to the Navidsons' new family home. It's a little unusual: you may discover that the house is bigger on the inside, with a maze of hallways and a forever-descending spiral staircase. Actually, you're not at the house. You're watching a documentary about the family, which becomes a documentary about the house. Or are you reading an academic text about said documentary, written by a man you've never met? You're definitely lost though, wandering down hallways of words and footnotes, and you may have to read some of it in a mirror. Might as well take another sip of the punch you poured yourself at the house. It's a bit of a mishmash, but so is the book you're reading. Or are you writing it? Or are you still in the Navidsons' home after all?

YIELD: 15 to 20 servings

1 (750 milliliter) bottle vodka

1 (750 milliliter) bottle rum

1 (750 milliliter) bottle triple sec

4 cups pineapple juice

2 cups orange juice

2 cups fruit punch or cranberry juice

1 cup simple syrup (adjust the amount to taste)

2 to 3 oranges, sliced

1 pound strawberries, washed and sliced

1. In a large punch bowl or beverage dispenser, combine the vodka, rum, and triple sec.
2. Pour in the pineapple juice, orange juice, fruit punch or cranberry juice, and simple syrup.
3. Stir the mixture well to ensure that all the ingredients are thoroughly combined.
4. Add the sliced oranges and strawberries to the mixture. These will not only boost flavor but also look appealing in the punch.
5. Allow the Jungle Juice to chill in the refrigerator for a few hours before serving. This allows the flavors to meld.
6. When you're ready to serve the punch, add ice cubes to the punch bowl or individual glasses.

WHITE RUSSIAN IS FOR WITCHING

White Is for Witching
by Helen Oyeyemi (2009)

A pile of white apples is set out for you in the kitchen, even though it isn't apple season. Chalk dust lines your coat pockets from the chalk pieces you've been eating. A mannequin comes to life and attacks the housekeeper. A sinister basement beckons you to stay in the house forever. All these fragmented horrors reside within the Silver House, a bed-and-breakfast haunted by generational trauma, which acts out against its inhabitants in grotesque ways. Best to keep your wits about you with this coffee-flavored cocktail, which hides its true alcoholic nature behind a wall of cream.

YIELD: 1 serving

2 ounces vodka

1 ounce coffee liqueur (for example, Kahlúa)

1 ounce heavy cream

a sprinkle of grated nutmeg (optional)

1. Fill a rocks glass with ice cubes.
2. Pour the vodka and coffee liqueur over the ice.
3. Pour the heavy cream slowly over the back of a spoon and onto the drink. Or drizzle the heavy cream over the top of the other ingredients. This creates a layered effect, with the cream floating on top.
4. Use a stirring stick or a spoon to gently stir the ingredients in the glass. This will help mix the flavors without fully incorporating the cream into the drink.
5. Garnish with grated nutmeg, if using.

THINGS WE MULLED IN THE CIDER

Things We Lost in the Fire
by Mariana Enriquez (2017)

Women set themselves aflame to combat the growing scourge of domestic violence. A tour guide is slowly stalked by the murderer whose crimes are the focus of his tours. A group of kids fascinated by a creepy house decide to go in, but do they come out? These tales woven together by Mariana Enriquez in Argentina hark back to the country's dark past to chill the soul. Warm yourself up while reading these terrifying stories with this spiced autumnal treat.

YIELD: 16 servings

1 gallon (about 4 liters) apple cider

1 orange, sliced

1 lemon, sliced

2 to 3 cinnamon sticks

6 to 8 whole cloves

1 or 2 star anise pods

½ cup brown sugar (adjust to taste)

1 to 2 inches of fresh ginger, sliced (optional)

1 cup dark rum, bourbon, or brandy (choose your favorite)

additional cinnamon sticks and orange or lemon slices, for garnish (optional)

1. In a large pot, combine the apple cider, orange and lemon slices, cinnamon sticks, whole cloves, star anise pods, brown sugar, and fresh ginger slices, if using.
2. Place the pot over medium heat, and bring the mixture to a gentle simmer. Avoid boiling the cider to preserve the flavors.
3. Allow the cider to simmer for at least 20 to 30 minutes to infuse the spices and blend the flavors. Simmer longer for a more intense flavor.
4. Taste the mulled cider and adjust the sweetness with more brown sugar if needed. Stir until the sugar dissolves.
5. Stir in 1 cup of your preferred alcohol: dark rum, bourbon, or brandy. Adjust the amount based on your preference for a stronger or milder spiked cider.
6. Optionally, strain the mulled cider to remove the solid spices and fruit slices, or serve the mulled cider with them for a rustic presentation.
7. Serve in mugs and garnish with additional cinnamon sticks and orange or lemon slices, if using.

THE BLOODY CHAMBORD

The Bloody Chamber by Angela Carter (1979)

In this short story collection, Angela Carter deftly retells romantic fairy tales with a heavily gothic twist. Carter weaves horror and romance together as she tells us her versions of "Sleeping Beauty," "Beauty and the Beast," "Little Red Riding Hood," and more. The titular story, "The Bloody Chamber," reexamines the grisly tale of Bluebeard, in which a young bride discovers the gruesome fates of her husband's previous wives. With this deliciously crimson-hued love potion cocktail, indulge in your fantasies of a grand castle with horrible secrets, heavy iron keys, and running through the gardens in a blood-stained gown.

YIELD: 1 serving

1½ ounces vodka (or your preferred base spirit)

1 ounce raspberry liqueur or Chambord

½ ounce peach schnapps

½ ounce cranberry juice

½ ounce pineapple juice

¼ ounce freshly squeezed lime juice

splash of soda water or club soda

fresh berries or edible flowers, for garnish

1. In a shaker, combine vodka or your preferred base spirit, raspberry liqueur or Chambord, peach schnapps, cranberry juice, pineapple juice, and lime juice.
2. Add ice to the shaker, and shake well to chill the mixture.
3. Strain the cocktail into an ice-filled glass.
4. Top with a splash of soda water or club soda for effervescence.
5. Garnish with fresh berries or edible flowers for a romantic touch.

LESTAT'S BLOODY SAZERAC

Interview with the Vampire
by Anne Rice (1976)

Immortality can be a real bummer after a while, at least for Louis, who has endured centuries of drama. Rewind two hundred years, and the diabolical Lestat is turning everyone in New Orleans into a vampire, including Louis and a child named Claudia. And then we get to the heart of the story: two vampire dads are trying to raise their vampire child in an ever-changing world. Hijinks abound obviously—and we didn't even get to the love triangle. Indulge your inner horny vampire with this bloody twist on a New Orleans staple, and hope that Lestat doesn't crash your party.

YIELD: 1 serving

1 sugar cube

red food coloring (optional)

2 ounces rye whiskey

3 dashes Peychaud's bitters

½ ounce raspberry liqueur (Chambord or similar)

absinthe or absinthe substitute, for rinsing

lemon peel, for garnish

1. Chill an old-fashioned glass by placing it in the freezer.
2. Place a sugar cube in the center of a mixing glass. Add a few drops of red food coloring to the sugar cube for a deep red hue, if using.
3. Pour the rye whiskey over the sugar cube. Allow it to soak into the cube for a moment.
4. Muddle the soaked sugar cube with the back of a spoon to dissolve it into the whiskey.
5. Add the Peychaud's bitters to the mixture.
6. Fill the mixing glass with ice cubes, and stir the ingredients well to chill the mixture.
7. Pour the raspberry liqueur (Chambord or similar) into the mixing glass.
8. Remove the ice from the chilled mixing glass.
9. Pour a small amount of absinthe or absinthe substitute into the chilled old-fashioned glass. Coat the interior by swirling the glass, then discard the excess.
10. Strain the chilled rye whiskey, sugar cube, bitters, and raspberry liqueur mixture into the chilled old-fashioned glass.
11. Express the oil from a lemon peel over the drink by giving it a twist over the glass.
12. Add the lemon peel to the glass as a garnish.

MEXICAN HOT GOTHOLATE

Mexican Gothic
by Silvia Moreno-Garcia (2020)

Glamorous party girl Noemí makes her way to an old home in the Mexican countryside to rescue her beloved cousin, who recently married into a strange English family. You're sure to feel a chill or two as you and Noemí explore the unnerving house and uncover the secrets within. And is there something . . . growing around the grounds? You'll need a comforting sip of Mexican hot chocolate to find your courage to discover just what is happening at High Place.

YIELD: 2 servings

2 cups whole milk

3 ounces dark chocolate (70% cocoa or higher), finely chopped

2 tablespoons granulated sugar (adjust to taste)

½ teaspoon ground cinnamon

¼ teaspoon ground nutmeg

¼ teaspoon chili powder, for a hint of heat (optional)

pinch of salt

½ teaspoon vanilla extract

whipped cream, cinnamon sticks, or additional cinnamon, for garnish (optional)

1. In a saucepan over medium heat, warm the milk until it's hot but not boiling.
2. Add the finely chopped dark chocolate to the milk, stirring continuously until the chocolate is completely melted and the mixture is smooth.
3. Add the sugar, ground cinnamon, ground nutmeg, chili powder (if using), and salt to the milk. Continue stirring until the ingredients are well combined.
4. Allow the hot chocolate to simmer for a few minutes, ensuring that it doesn't boil. Simmering helps infuse the flavors.
5. Remove the saucepan from the heat, and stir in the vanilla extract.
6. Taste the hot chocolate and adjust the sweetness and spice levels to your liking by adding more sugar or spices if needed.
7. Pour the Mexican hot chocolate into mugs, and garnish with whipped cream, a cinnamon stick, or a sprinkle of cinnamon on top of each mug, if using.

HER BRANDY AND OTHER PARTIES

Her Body and Other Parties
by Carmen Maria Machado (2017)

Girl meets boy. They fall in love. Girl has a mysterious ribbon around her neck. Boy really wants to know what this ribbon is about. They get married and have a son. Both men are consumed with longing for her untouchable ribbon. This collection of short stories only gets spookier from there. What if *Law & Order: SVU* were reimagined into a surreal television show filled with ghosts, aliens, and doppelgängers? Carmen Maria Machado is a master of horror, and her refreshing short story collection calls on archetypal gothic tropes to explore horrible truths in these modern stories. Why not pair one of these short stories with an inspired reimagining of a cocktail classic? If you don't, then you risk the heady truths of these tales overwhelming your fragile psyche. This contemporary take on a brandy stinger has a twist of decadence with the addition of chocolate liqueur. For the traditionalist, skip the chocolate liqueur.

YIELD: 1 serving

2 ounces brandy

1 ounce white crème de menthe

½ ounce chocolate liqueur (such as Godiva or crème de cacao) (optional)

fresh mint leaves, for garnish (optional)

chocolate shavings, for garnish (optional)

1. Combine the brandy, white crème de menthe, and chocolate liqueur (if using) in an ice-filled cocktail shaker.
2. Shake well until chilled, about 15 to 20 seconds.
3. Strain the mixture into a chilled cocktail glass.
4. Garnish with fresh mint leaves and sprinkle with chocolate shavings, if using.

DRINKS INDEX

BOOK INDEX

ACKNOWLEDGMENTS

Thank you to everyone who helped this spooky little book get published. Everyone at Ulysses Press deserves all the chills and thrills, particularly: Casie Vogel, for being a creepy cheerleader every day; Shelona Belfon, for being very gentle with deadlines; the beautiful designers of this book, Akangksha Sarmah and Winnie Liu; and photographer Nevyana Dimitrova, who understood my dark desires perfectly.

I would also like to thank my family, who put up with months of painful puns. I owe you many macabre drinks.

Thank you, of course, to the genre of gothic fiction. Without you, my nightmares would be uninspired and my cocktails would be far less spirited.

And finally, thank you to the wonderful readers. May you always have a good book to read.

ABOUT THE AUTHOR

IPHIGENIA JONES has seen every episode of *The Addams Family* and has been accused of witchcraft only thrice. She enjoys cats, blackberries, and chatting with ghosts.